In the Shelter of His Wings

Resting in God's
Tender Care

PAINTINGS BY Carolyn Shores Wright

HARVEST HOUSE PUBLISHERS

EUGENE, OREGON

In The Shelter of His Wings

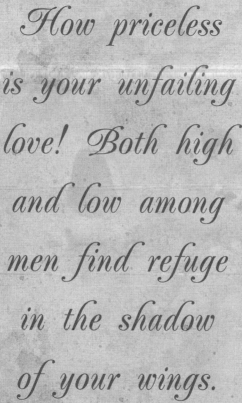

How priceless is your unfailing love! Both high and low among men find refuge in the shadow of your wings.

PSALM 36:7

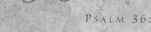

3

God has not promised skies always blue,

Flower-strewn pathways all our lives through;

God has not promised sun without rain,

Joy without sorrow, peace without pain.

But God has promised strength for the day,

Rest for the labor, light for the way,

Grace for the trials, help from above,

Unfailing sympathy, undying love.

Annie Johnson Flint

6

The glory of life is
to love, not to be
loved; to give, not
to get; to serve, not
to be served. Love
is the true miracle,
and to the one who
loves come both
wonder and joy.

HUGH BLACK

*He who dwells in
the shelter of the
Most High will
rest in the shadow
of the Almighty.*

PSALM 91:1

7

Take the name of Jesus with you,

Child of sorrow and of woe,

It will joy and comfort give you;

Take it then, where'er you go.

LYDIA BAXTER

An infinite God can give all of Himself to each of His children.

He does not distribute Himself that each may have a part, but to

each one He gives all of Himself as fully as if there were no others.

A.W. Tozer

Carolyn Shores Wright

Carolyn Shores Wright

God does not lead His children around hardship, but leads them straight through hardship. But He leads! And amidst the hardship, He is nearer to them than ever before.

OTTO DIBELIUS

Keep working your way through the maze. You'll know what it is when it happens, but you won't know until then. "God grinds the axes he intends to use."

DAVE SIM

11

Pain is inevitable. Suffering is optional.

M. KATHLEEN CASEY

Character cannot be developed
in ease and quiet. Only through
experiences of trial and suffering
can the soul be strengthened,
vision cleared, ambition inspired
and success achieved.

Helen Keller

Faith goes up the stairs that love has built and
looks out the window which hope has opened.

CHARLES SPURGEON

Carolyn Jantes Wright

Carolyn Shores Wright ©

I do not ask to walk smooth paths nor bear an easy load.

I pray for strength and fortitude to climb the rock strewn road.

Give me such courage and I can scale the hardest peaks alone,

And transform every stumbling block into a stepping stone.

GALE BROOK BURKET

15

God stirs up our comfortable
nests, and pushes us over the
edge of them, and we are
forced to use our wings to
save ourselves from fatal
falling. Read your trials in this
light, and see if your wings
are being developed.

HANNAH WHITALL SMITH

God comforts us on every side.

PSALM 71:21

God is in control
of all outcomes as
well as in control
of the process.

MERILYN THOMPSON

Encouragement is oxygen to the soul.

GEORGE M. ADAMS

You will never understand
why God does what He
does, but if you believe
Him, that is all that is
necessary. Let us learn
to trust for who He Is.

Elisabeth Elliot

I long. . . to take refuge in the
shelter of your wings.

Psalm 61:4

His love has no limit, His grace has no measure,

His power has no boundary known unto men;

For out of His infinite riches in Jesus

He giveth, and giveth, and giveth again!

Annie Johnson Flint

Isn't the breath of the mint delicious?
And that tea rose—why, it's a song
and a hope and a prayer all in one.

L.M. MONTGOMERY

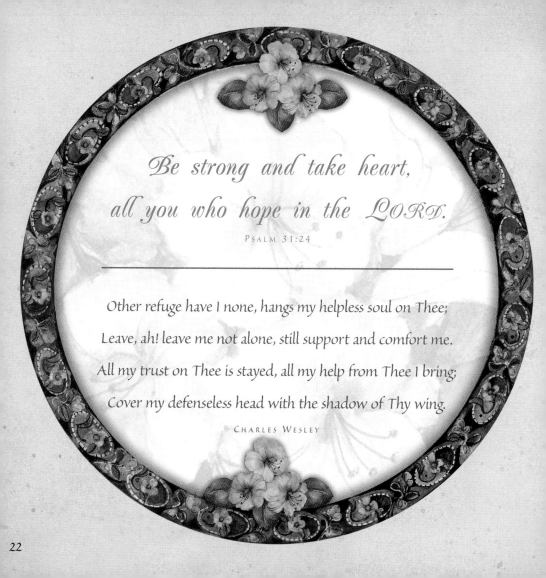

Be strong and take heart,
all you who hope in the LORD.

PSALM 31:24

Other refuge have I none, hangs my helpless soul on Thee;

Leave, ah! leave me not alone, still support and comfort me.

All my trust on Thee is stayed, all my help from Thee I bring;

Cover my defenseless head with the shadow of Thy wing.

CHARLES WESLEY

23

Just when my hopes are vanished,

Just when my friends forsake,

Just when the fight is thickest,

Just when with fear I shake—

Then comes a still, small whisper:

"Fear not, My child, I'm near."

Jesus brings peace and comfort,

I love His voice to hear.

J. BRUCE EVANS

Jesus Christ is the same yesterday and today and forever.

HEBREWS 13:8

Are we weak and heavy laden, cumbered with a load of care?

Precious Savior, still our refuge; take it to the Lord in prayer:

Do thy friends despise, forsake thee? Take it to the Lord in prayer;

In His arms He'll take and shield thee; thou will find a solace there.

Joseph Scriven

Carolyn Shores Wright

28

Under His wings, what a refuge in sorrow!

How the heart yearningly turns to His rest!

Often when earth has no balm for my healing,

There I find comfort, and there I am blessed.

WILLIAM CUSHING

Blessed be the God of all comfort.

2 CORINTHIANS 1:3

You are a hiding place for me;

you preserve me from trouble;

you surround me with glad

cries of deliverance.

PSALM 32:7 NRSV

All the art of living lies in a fine

...mingling of letting go and holding on.

HENRY HAVELOCK ELLIS

Who will tell whether one happy
moment of love or the joy of
breathing or walking on a bright
morning and smelling the fresh
air, is not worth all the suffering
and effort which life implies.

Erich Fromm

The LORD is close to
the brokenhearted
and saves those who
are crushed in spirit.

PSALM 34:18

*I will turn
their mourning
into joy,
and will
comfort them.*

JEREMIAH 31:13 NASB

33

Let us then approach the throne of grace with confidence, so that we may receive mercy and find grace to help us in our time of need.

HEBREWS 4:16

34

My heart is filled with happiness

And sweet rejoicing, too.

To walk with God is perfect peace,

A joy forever new.

Author Unknown

©91 Carolyn Shores Wright

Regardless of the circumstance,

Regardless of the fear,

Regardless of the pain we bear,

Regardless of the tear,

Our God is ever in control,

Performing as He should,

And He has promised in His Word

To work things for our good.

But as a loving Father would,

He sometimes lets us cry

To cleanse the hurt out of our heart,

To wash it from our eye.

Yet gently gathers He the tears

Within His hands to stay

Until He turns them into pearls

And gives them back someday.

GLENDA FULTON DAVIS

38

If someone listens, or

stretches out a hand, or

whispers a word of

encouragement, or

attempts to understand

a lonely person,

extraordinary things

begin to happen.

LORETTA GIRZARTIS

At the heart of the cyclone tearing the sky

And flinging the clouds and the towers by,

Is a place of central calm;

So here in the roar of mortal things,

I have a place where my spirit sings,

In the hollow of God's palm.

Edwin Markham

This is that "peace of God which passeth all understanding"...It

is a peace which all the powers of earth and hell are unable to

take from him. Waves and storms beat upon it, but they shake

it not; for it is founded upon a rock. It keeps the hearts and

minds of the children of God, at all times and in all places.

John Wesley

The lightning was flashing, the thunder was roaring, the wind was blowing; but the little bird was asleep in the crevice of the rock, its head serenely under its wing, sound asleep. That is peace: to be able to rest serenely in the storm.

BILLY GRAHAM

41

Carolyn Shores Wright

42

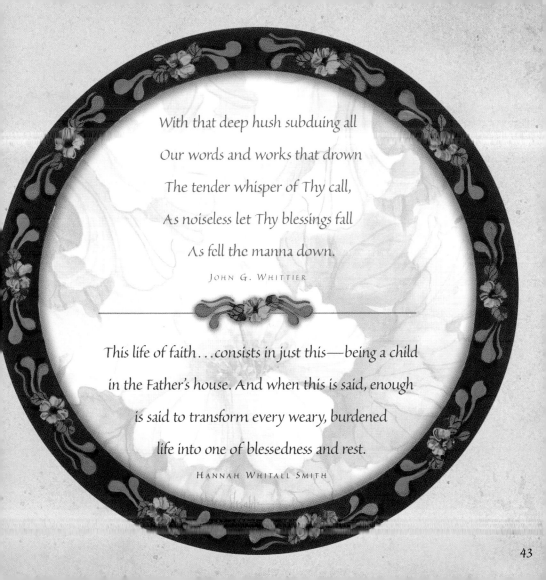

With that deep hush subduing all

Our words and works that drown

The tender whisper of Thy call,

As noiseless let Thy blessings fall

As fell the manna down.

JOHN G. WHITTIER

This life of faith…consists in just this—being a child

in the Father's house. And when this is said, enough

is said to transform every weary, burdened

life into one of blessedness and rest.

HANNAH WHITALL SMITH

I will ask the Father
and he will give you
another Comforter,
and he will never
leave you. He is the
Holy Spirit, the
Spirit who leads
into all truth.

JOHN 14:16-17 TLB

*My depths are held by peace. The surface
may be disturbed; it's the depths that count.*

E. STANLEY JONES

Rest is not a hallowed feeling that comes over us in church; it is the repose of a heart set deep in God.

HENRY DRUMMOND

Carolyn Shores Wright ©79

46

The thought on which I delight to dwell, as I advance in life, is that God is within me— always present to my soul, to teach, to rebuke, to aid, to bless…and in the feeling of God's intimate presence with this, to enlighten, quicken, and save, I find strength, and hope, and peace.

WILLIAM ELLERY CHANNING

47

Carolyn Thores Wright

To endure all things with an equable
and peaceful mind, not only brings
with it many blessings to the soul,
but also enables us, in the midst
of our difficulties, to have a clear
judgment about them, and to
minister the fitting remedy for them.

ST. JOHN OF THE CROSS

The Lord is in control. He has
forgiven the past, He is in charge of now,
and shows the way for each new day.

DR. LLOYD JOHN OGILVIE

Be strong and courageous. Do not
be terrified; do not be discouraged,
for the LORD your God will be with
you wherever you go.

JOSHUA 1:9

50

That's how it is with the "God of peace." Instead of hanging on with growing despair and weakening fingers, you see the adequate resources and the infinite wisdom of your God at work, and you learn to be content because of what He is doing and the way He's doing it.

STUART BRISCOE

51

With eager heart and will on fire,

I strove to win my great desire.

"Peace shall be mine," I said; but life

Grew bitter in the barren strife.

My soul was weary, and my pride

Was wounded deep; to Heaven I cried,

"God grant me peace or I must die;"

The dumb stars glittered no reply.

Broken at last, I bowed my head,

Forgetting all myself, and said,

"Whatever comes, His will be done;"

And in that moment peace was won.

Henry van Dyke

Carolyn Shores Wright

53

*God has ventured all in Jesus
Christ to save us, now He
wants us to venture our all in
abandoned confidence in Him.*

OSWALD CHAMBERS

"I am leaving you with a gift—peace
of mind and heart! And the peace I
give isn't fragile like the world gives.
So don't be troubled or afraid."

JOHN 14:27 TLB

Carolyn Shores Wright ©96

Do not be anxious about anything, but in everything, by prayer

and petition, with thanksgiving, present your requests to God.

And the peace of God, which transcends all understanding,

will guard your hearts and your minds in Christ Jesus.

PHILIPPIANS 4:6-7

There's a peace in my heart that the world never gave,

A peace it cannot take away;

Tho' the trials of life may surround like a cloud,

I've a peace that has come there to stay.

MRS. WILL L. MURPHY

The Extravagance of God

More sky than man can see,

More seas than he can sail,

More sun than he can bear to watch,

More stars than he can scale.

More breath than he can breathe,

More yield than he can sow,

More grace than he can comprehend,

More love than he can know.

Ralph W. Seager

We shall steer safely through
every storm, so long as our
heart is right, our intention
fervent, our courage steadfast,
and our trust fixed on God.

ST. FRANCIS DE SALES

Be still, and know that I am God.

PSALM 46:10

"I have told you these things, so that in me you may have peace. In this world you will have trouble. But take heart! I have overcome the world."

JOHN 16:33

Praise be to the God and Father of our Lord Jesus Christ, the Father of compassion and the God of all comfort, who comforts us in all our troubles, so that we can comfort those in any trouble with the comfort we ourselves have received from God.

2 CORINTHIANS 1:3-4

Because you are my help,

I sing in the shadow of your wings.

PSALM 63:7